SUMMER

—— A ——
TIME
—— TO ——
ENJOY

$SEASONS$ OF $LIFE$

SUMMER

— A —

TIME

TO

ENJOY

$MEDITATIONS$

Bernie Sheahan

Thomas Nelson Publishers
NASHVILLE

Published in Nashville, Tennessee, by Janet Thoma Books, a division of Thomas Nelson Publishers, Inc., and distributed in Canada by Word Communications, Ltd., Richmond, British Columbia, and in the United Kingdom by Word (UK), Ltd., Milton Keynes, England.

Unless otherwise indicated, Scripture quotations are from the NEW KING JAMES VERSION of the Bible. Copyright © 1979, 1980, 1982, Thomas Nelson, Inc., Publishers.

Library of Congress Cataloging-in-Publication Data

Sheahan, Bernie.
     Summer: a time to enjoy / by Bernie Sheahan.
          p.   cm.
     ISBN 0-8407-9278-6
     1. Summer—Religious aspects—Christianity—Meditations.
2. Devotional calendars. I. Title.
BV4832.2.S499   1994
242—dc20   93–2274
                                                              CIP

Printed in the United States of America
1 2 3 4 — 97 96 95 94

To everything there is a season,
A time for every purpose under heaven:
A time to be born,
And a time to die;
A time to plant,
And a time to pluck what is planted;
A time to kill,
And a time to heal;
A time to break down,
And a time to build up;
A time to weep,
And a time to laugh;
A time to mourn,
And a time to dance;
A time to cast away stones,
And a time to gather stones;
A time to embrace,
And a time to refrain from embracing;
A time to gain,
And a time to lose;
A time to keep,
And a time to throw away;
A time to tear,
And a time to sew;
A time to keep silence,
And a time to speak;
A time to love,
And a time to hate;
A time of war,
And a time of peace.

Ecclesiastes 3:1–8

To Dad, Mom, Jer, the Avilas, and Sheahans,
for the summer stories

to Laura Frances, for seeing me through

and to Mom, for the gift of words.

To Everything There Is a Season

The seasons of life are more than spring, summer, fall, and winter. There is a season when you prepare for childbirth, and a season for saying good-bye to a loved one. There is the season of working hard for financial security, and there is the season of smelling roses and walking hand in hand with a loved one.

A season is not defined as much by an increment of time or the changing landscape as it is by a lesson learned or wisdom gained. And with each new season you will need a new set of skills and strengths. You will need endurance to face childbirth, and understanding to help you grieve a loss. Patience and determination will be essential as you climb the corporate ladder, and peace and joy will accompany you as you walk with your partner through all the fields of life.

The *Seasons of Life Meditations* were created to be a friend traveling with you as you experience the joys and sorrows of each season. They will console, energize, counsel, chide, and inspire. These meditations contain the gentle wisdom of those who have experienced many seasons of their own. While they may not completely understand your situation, the authors have been somewhere similar and can offer advice to help you understand yourself, your emotions, God, and your world.

The authors and editors wish you peace, wisdom, and love as you face all of your *Seasons of Life.*

> *Live in each season as it passes;*
> *breathe the air, drink the drink, taste*
> *the fruit, and resign yourself to the*
> *influences of each.*
> —Henry David Thoreau

*P*erhaps more than any other season, summer gives us the opportunity to just "be," to slow down and live, instead of merely surviving from activity to activity. For those of us with kids, summer can mean an entire three months without PTA meetings, school plays, and football practice. . . maybe even a glorious week or two when the kids are away at camp! And for those who are single and working, the longer days of summer beckon us to come home, slip into shorts and sneakers, and make the most of warm evenings spent with family or friends.

Is there a way you can resign yourself to the influences of summer? Maybe this is the time to start those tennis lessons you've been meaning to take and work up a good sweat two nights a week. Or find out if there's a drive-in theater still around and pile the family into the station wagon for a fun night out. How about inviting those new neighbors over for burgers on the patio?

Could it be that the best way to enjoy life right now is to do nothing? It's okay to do that, you know. You might even want to splurge on a new hammock, make yourself some lemonade, and spend one of these warm summer evenings suspended between two trees! Breathe the air. Drink the drink. Taste the fruit. Let go and let yourself enjoy the pleasures of the season.

Get the most out of summer.

The grass always looks greener on the other side.

$\mathscr{R}$emember February? Cold, damp, dreary; bare trees and dirty snow; endless rain; cloudy days that seem to last a lifetime. You were tired of muddy boots messing up your kitchen floor, or having to wash endless loads of laundry just to keep everyone in layers of clean, warm clothes. The kids may have had fun in the snow, but you found yourself saying, "I can't wait for summer!"

Now it's summer and you're growing weary of the heat, day in and day out, with no relief in sight except for afternoon naps in the air-conditioned house. The pavement's too hot for bare feet, mosquitoes ruin the summer nights, and you actually look forward to a nice, crisp February day.

Sounds like a clear-cut case of the grass being greener on the other side! Isn't it possible just to enjoy the day that's put before us without wishing we were somewhere else?

Of course it is. But sometimes it takes a real effort to get our feelings to catch up with the truth. That's why we need to focus every day on what we've been given for this day, complete with its joys and sorrows, delights and irritations. There's a way to do that, but not without help. It's called grace, and we need it just as much when life is monotonous as when it's painful or full of pressure.

Today I will embrace what is given to me without complaining. I know that even the monotony of a long, hot summer day can remind me to take hold of the present, without wishing it away for something I think would be better.

April showers bring May flowers but June weddings bring April showers.

It's June again, and that means weddings. Those who are in a good marriage can enjoy going to a wedding and remembering their own "happiest day." What about those who've been divorced? A wedding can serve as a painful reminder of broken vows and unfulfilled dreams.

Some may attend a wedding and feel the sharp twinge of pain from a broken engagement, a marriage that almost was. The peculiar loneliness of being single and longing for intimacy with a life partner can make it hard to rejoice in the happiness of yet another married couple.

Any of these things can make it hard to shop for a wedding gift, attend a bridal shower, or even hear the strains of Mendelssohn's *Wedding March*. Weddings are packed with emotions, whether they are pleasure, pain, or a mixture of both.

Next time you go to a wedding, focus on your emotions. Ask God to help you accept your circumstance, whatever it is.

School days, school days, dear old Golden Rule days . . .

It seems that no matter how old we get or how long it was since our last school day, June somehow brings back some of the same feelings that it used to give us, knowing that we were at the end of a long academic year. I remember those last few days of anticipation, counting the hours until we were free at last, cramming for those final exams, and looking forward to emancipation from studies. Now, as the days get warmer and the graduation greeting cards fill the store racks, I still get a sense of excitement, even though my daily work schedule doesn't change a bit.

It's no wonder that we experience a little of that considering that most of us spent twelve, sixteen, or even more of our formative years waiting for school to be out in the summer. It's a natural function of our "inner clock," and it's enhanced by the fact that we all know someone—maybe our own children—who is excited about summer vacation.

So what do we do with those feelings? Most of us experience few changes as dramatic as getting out of school, unless we're teachers or students. But can we take advantage of that "inner clock" to make some beneficial changes in our lives? How about setting out to do something different during summer vacation, like planning a weekend getaway, joining a softball team, or planting a garden? Maybe we can recapture some of that old June vitality and put it to good use.

Think about what it felt like to get out of school for summer vacation. Then write down three things you can do this summer to change your daily pattern and bring back some of that youthful exuberance. Tell somebody about it.

*Let the little children come to Me,
and do not forbid them; for of such
is the kingdom of heaven.*

—*Matthew 19:14*

When was the last time you took off your shoes and played in the sprinkler? Or took advantage of a summer rainshower and walked around the block, letting yourself get soaked to the skin? "I can't do that anymore; I'm a responsible adult." Yes, and you're probably missing out on the pure delight of being a kid. Watch the children next time you're in a park. Do they worry about what people will think? Of course not. That's something that we learn as we get older and gradually "put away childish things," as the apostle Paul said in the New Testament letter to the Corinthians.

Is that what Paul meant? I doubt it! Put away immaturity, maybe. Leave behind elementary ideas of faith as you grow in your journey, probably. But if Jesus Christ himself told his followers to "come unto me as little children," then there must be something to the idea of maintaining childlike wonder and spontaneity. Children respond naturally to beauty and joy, and they don't hold back when they are excited about something. They possess an inner freedom that permits them to be outwardly enthusiastic about life without fear of criticism.

Wouldn't it be great to get some of that back? What if you threw caution to the wind and took a walk in the rain, or climbed a tree for no good reason, or went to the park and hopped on a swing? Sure, you might get a strange look from somebody, but who cares? You're a grown-up, and you can do anything you want to.

Lord, help me today to see life through the eyes of a child. Instead of attempting to look perfect, help me to give myself the grace to be spontaneous and free in my enjoyment of your world.

*When a person that one loves is in
the world and alive and well . . .
then to miss them is only a new
flavor, a salt sharpness in
experience.*

—Winifred Holtby

For me, summer is a time of remembering people I love—people who are far away because a season of our lives is over. During June, July, and August I can recall the in-between time at Mom and Dad's, as a college student living in a home that was no longer really mine, working at a summer job to make money for next year's school expenses. Mid-June reminds me of graduation day and saying farewell to college friends. And the "dog days" of late summer bring back memories of leaving friends and family and taking a new job 2,000 miles away.

That was more than a dozen years ago, and despite the fact that I've made friends as dear as the ones I left behind, I still miss the ones who shared my early years. While it's true that, like the seasons, friendships come and go, a few stay near in heart, if not in proximity.

But it takes effort to maintain and nurture those long-distance relationships. An occasional phone call, a card, or a letter is like a deposit in a bank account, an investment in caring that accrues over time. Remembering friends in a tangible way says "you are important to me." I'm reminded of that funny little song we used to sing in Girl Scouts: "Make new friends, but keep the old, one is silver and the other's gold." Simple, maybe, but true. Friends who've known us through the seasons of our lives are worth their weight in gold, and more.

Think of one friend who is far away. Take the time today to write a little note or pick up the phone, just to let them know you miss them.

When all else fails, read the map.

One of my favorite summer activities is taking long road trips. The longer the better, and if I'm not in a hurry to reach my destination, the trip is that much more fun.

I have an old road atlas that I was given more than a dozen years ago for a cross-country trip. Sometimes, when I'm feeling restless, I'll take that atlas out and reminisce about trips I've taken and dream about trips to come. I've been doing that a lot lately! My "cabin fever" gets pretty severe during winter, and the warm days of spring and early summer start my driving foot to itching.

As I write this, I'm longing for wide open spaces and big skies, so I'm thinking about a trip to Colorado in mid-summer. How do I get there? Without looking at the map, I know I head west, but that's as far as I get. Which interstate do I take? What states will I travel through, and what cities will I visit? Are there places along the way that I'll want to see?

When I look at the map, I see that I have plenty of choices, as long as I go west. Direction is the key element in my decision making.

I suppose life is like that. In order to get where

I want to go, I have to set my sights on a goal, a destination. In my case, I want to follow God's road map for my life. And that means making a lot of choices along the way. Guided by God's word, the wisdom of people I trust, and the inner workings of God's spirit, I can have confidence that I will make it to the place where I want to go.

Write down one "destination" you want to include in your spiritual journey. Share it with a friend or your spouse, and talk about how to get there.

> *At the moment, our bodies are continually responding to the messages from our minds. So what messages is your mind giving your body?*
>
> —*Margo Adair*

*Y*ikes! It's swimsuit season again. What happened? I meant to be thinner by this time! I meant to spend March, April, and May working out at the gym and eating nothing but alfalfa sprouts and raw carrots! Whoops . . . *I forgot.* I forgot that ice cream and pizza and bean burritos are not weight-reducing items. I *forgot* that sitting down all winter and spring tends to put on the pounds, and that in order to slim down, one needs to get off one's duff to see any results.

It's not that bad, really—I'm exaggerating. But the older I get, the more I realize that Sir Isaac Newton really had something with that gravity idea because gravity is taking its toll on my person.

But does it really matter? Magazines and billboards scream a not-so-subtle message that if we aren't slim and trim, we aren't desirable. If we don't have our bodies under control, our lives must be out of control. There's something wrong with us. And though this message used to be aimed at women, all you have to do is look at *GQ* or *Esquire* to know that men are under pressure to have perfect bodies, too.

It's one thing to be concerned about health, to eat things that are good for us, and to get enough exercise to keep ourselves reasonably fit. But do we have to be slaves to a cultural ideal that demands conformity? Of course not. *Just say no.*

This summer, I will try not to be overly concerned with the way I look. I will rely on God to help me withstand the pressure to be perfect.

Carpe diem—"Seize the day."

I was captivated by those words when I first saw the film *Dead Poets Society*. If you saw it, they probably captivated you, too. Robin Williams was the boarding school English teacher, urging his students to look into the faces in the faded photographs, the ones who had gone before them many years ago. *"Carpe diem,"* they are saying—"Seize the day."

I remember a summer day just a few years ago. I was sitting at the top of the stairs in the Kansas farmhouse where my father, his father, and his father's father all lived. Now a fourth generation is growing up in that house, and my little cousin Angela is one of those lucky ones who treads the same oak stairs our ancestors trod.

Angela may be young, but I think she understands what *carpe diem* means. At the top of those stairs, we sat together as she showed me a framed sepia-toned photograph of our great-grandmother and her family. "Her name was Sarah Scott," Angela reminded me, pointing out a young woman wearing a stiff Victorian collar and high-button shoes. "My sister is named after her."

Does Angela hear the voices, through the generations, over the years? She might not be able to articulate it that way, but I think she does. Can you "hear the voices" of your ancestors? Can you look into their ancient eyes and see the dreams they had for you?

Find a picture of one of your forebears, someone you never knew. Look at the face and imagine what his or her life was like. Then write a note to a future descendant of yours, telling him or her something about you.

Perseverance. Your own built-in taskmaster. The thing that makes you stick with a job until it's done.

*S*ummer, I believe, is the worst season of the year for timely completion of tasks. Summer is the time when you take your shoes off as often as possible, leave work as early as possible, and head for the lake or beach as soon as possible.

What seems less than possible, at least for me, is getting things done. I'd much rather swim, play softball, sit on the porch, hike up a mountain, mow the yard—anything but sit at a computer screen. So what do I do in this laziest of seasons when a project glares at me from across the desk? I usually succumb to temptation, especially if it involves ice cream.

But there is this thing called perseverance. It's a quality I've been short on most of my life, which is why summer school was never a good idea for me. Part of not persevering is the fear of the task, which for buttoned-down, straight-line, Type A people is usually not the issue. For those of us a little to the right brain of Type A, fear of the task can grow until the task itself takes on gargantuan proportions.

Perseverance doesn't listen when the task is

growling—it just keeps on doing what needs to be done.

The quote at the top of the page was clipped out of a magazine and given to me by my seventh-grade English teacher, Mrs. Dummler. She found that and thought of me. I guess I must not have been finishing my tasks very well. I don't have the clipping anymore, but I've never forgotten what it said and what its existence said about Mrs. Dummler as a caring teacher.

Guess what, Mrs. Dummler. I finally wrote a book.

I will stick to my important tasks today and get them done. Then I'll give myself a pat on the back.

. . . .

> *Hold a true friend with both hands.*
> —*Nigerian proverb*

*C*an you remember your first friend? Mine was a little dark-haired girl named LeeAnn, whose parents owned the beach cottage next-door to ours. I spent my earliest summers in that beach house in New Hampshire, and having LeeAnn as a playmate made those summer days just that much more fun. I've seen a picture of the two of us, tanned from long afternoons in the sun, bundled in sweaters to protect us from the evening chill as we played on the seesaw down by the water.

But even though LeeAnn and I were buddies, we couldn't possibly know what it meant to be a real friend. Life wasn't complicated enough to require that kind of relationship yet. Even so, I learned what real friendship was all about from my mom and her friend, Hilda, one warm night there at Hampton Beach. Friends since high school days, these two women strolled along the beach with their children in tow and talked for what seemed like hours. After a long day at the beach and an extra long walk down the board-walk, I was pooped. Wasn't Mommy tired?

Not tired enough to miss out on some special time with her friend. So us kids got put to bed

. . . .

and left with Grandma while Mommy and Hilda went for yet another walk. I didn't understand it then, but it left its mark on me. These days, Mom and Hilda have to make do with letters because years go by in between walks on the beach.

As for me, I've taken a lot of long walks on the beach with special people in my life. Now I stay up late and talk with dear friends whenever possible. I guess I have Mom and Hilda to thank for that.

Do you have a friend you'd like to stay up late with and talk to? Do it, if you can. Or call that friend and let her or him know you wish you could.

*Today a new sun rises for me;
everything lives, everything is
animated, everything seems to speak
to me of my passion, everything
invites me to cherish it.*

—Anne De Lenclos

I am drawn to people who have a real passion for life, a zest for adventure, and a flair for spontaneity. I like to live life on the edge, dance in the street if I hear a brass band, let the ice cream drip on my chin, eat watermelon with my hands and spit the seeds out afterward.

I like to have fun and to find it in the moment instead of looking for it elsewhere. I love to drink deep of earth's pleasures, talk about the meaning of life over a cup of tea or strong coffee, and pray and laugh with equal abandon. I want to be moved to tears by the rhythm of well-written words, to laughter by the timing of well-delivered comedy, and to action by the fervor of a well-preached sermon. I love the feel of the wheel, the hum of the engine, and the view from the open window. I brake for historical markers, old barns, and bunny rabbits with white cotton tails. I sing of mountains, oceans, and tender hearts. And when I go to the beach, I couldn't care less if it's raining—I will run and dive headlong into the waves, laughing all the way.

Come, play with me, and you are a kindred spirit and friend for life.

Do you know what you love? Have you ever written it down? Take the time to do it—find out what a delightful person you are.

I am a terrific person to know! Before today is through, I will take some time to write down the things that make me unique.

Laissez bon temps roulee—Let the good times roll!

One of my favorite summer events is something called the Golden Scoop. As you can imagine, this is an event that has something to do with that most sublime pleasure of summer: ice cream. My friend Billy, a certifiable ice cream addict (and a man after my own heart), offers his home, his boat-shaped wooden deck, and his collection of antique ice cream scoops to a circle of his closest friends. It happens every year in June, and though I am sworn to secrecy on the details of the Golden Scoop ceremony, I can tell you that it is a celebration that the F.O.B. (Friends of Billy) look forward to with great anticipation and delight.

Oh, there are grilled hamburgers, of course, and baked beans and potato salad. This is an official summer event, you know. But the high point of the evening is the ceremony, which is carried out with much pomp and silliness and serves to officially usher in the beginning of the ice cream season. Mind you, it would be great to have homemade ice cream, even without the party and the hilarity of the sacred ceremony. But it wouldn't be a celebration, and that's what makes it so special. I am glad to have friends who consider celebration to be such an important part of life. Whether the event honors a significant milestone, like a job promotion or a wedding engagement, or just commemorates the beginning of ice cream season, it's always accompanied by exuberant toasts, blessings, and sometimes a song or two. It's terrific!

Do you "celebrate the moments of your life?" Next time you've got something to celebrate, have a party.

Celebrations bring joy to life. I will take the time to celebrate even the small things this summer.

Living things need room to grow.

*H*aving come from a long line of farmers, I have a built-in affinity for growing things. I'm not much of a gardener, mind you, but my little suburban vegetable patch can still teach me a lot about life from a farmer's perspective. There are parables to learn from every trip out to the patch . . . every time I plant, water, yank weeds, or pull new vegetables from the ground.

One such parable I learned from Bell peppers—really! The instructions on the little white stake tell you exactly how far apart to plant the peppers for maximum growth. Put them too close, and they choke each other, with roots tangled and leaves fighting for space to grow. Plant them too far apart and you've wasted a lot of space, so you won't enjoy as many peppers. But plant them just right and they'll have enough room to spread their little stalks to the sun, enough area to absorb the rain, and a healthy share of the soil's nutrients below the surface.

Like the peppers, relationships need space to grow. Do you feel choked because someone wants to be too close? Maybe you're the one doing the choking. It may be a romantic relationship, a friendship, or a family relationship. For whatever reason—poor self-esteem, a desire for control, or unsatisfied emotional needs—relationships may get entangled to a point where those involved are dying instead of growing. And the disentangling process can be very painful, sometimes to the point of having to reach down and tear out roots in order to replant. How much better it would be to be planted together with enough room to grow in the first place!

I will give thought to my closest relationships. Do I have plenty of growing room? If not, I will think about ways to create healthy space.

Earth's crammed with heaven
And every common bush afire with
God;
But only he who sees takes off his
shoes,
The rest sit round it and pluck
blackberries.
    —*Elizabeth Barrett Browning*

If you've never read the book, then maybe you've seen Cecil B. DeMille's epic movie *The Ten Commandments*. Do you remember the scene when Moses went to the top of the mountain to meet with God? Moses met the Almighty in the form of a burning bush, and he was informed by the voice of God that where he was standing was holy ground. His response was that of reverence, awe, and holy fear; he took off his shoes.

The Japanese know about reverence and respect; they take off their shoes when they enter a house. It's not something we Americans do out of any particular courtesy. if we do it at all, it's to be comfortable or because our feet hurt. I love what Browning says in her poem. All around us is God's creation, earth crammed with heaven. Do we really respect it, revere it, and hold it in awe? Or do we simply take it for granted?

We live in a time of great awareness of Earth's

frailty. Some say that if we don't do something radical, we won't be able to pass on all its beauty to our descendants. Most of us do more than ever to make adjustments to help the earth—recycling, buying eco-friendly products, and generally "thinking green."

Some take concern for the environment to the extreme by worshiping nature. As a Christian, I can't buy that. But to revere the earth and its beauty as the wondrous work of God, to honor its loveliness with awe—that's something I can take my shoes off for.

O Lord, I will respect the earth out of gratitude for its beauty and wonder.

> *The mere sense of living is joy*
> *enough.*
> —Emily Dickinson

I am fortunate to have a veranda where I live. It's an upstairs porch really, but "veranda" makes me sound like Scarlett O'Hara, doesn't it? I live on a quiet little street where most of the houses were built in the 1930s. Back then, they didn't have air conditioning, which is why houses had porches. Families could sit outside on summer nights when it was too hot to be indoors. That made for much conversation and the telling of stories because there's not much else to do when you're sitting on a porch. Rocking chairs and porch swings were places to "sit a spell" and visit.

Being out on the front porch gave you a connection to your neighbors—after all, they stepped off their porch, down their front walk, up the sidewalk, and to your house. Walking down the street in the evening, you could greet neighbors sitting on their porches, and maybe stop to have an iced tea and catch up on the latest news.

It's still that way in my neighborhood. I suspect that people who choose to live in old houses with front porches do so because they like to sit on them in the summer and talk to the neighbors.

I imagine that all of us, whether we have one on our house or not, know the pleasure of porch-sitting. Maybe it was Grandma's house, or that big lodge up in the mountains, or that old place by the lake. It's hard to beat the feeling of just sitting and rocking and letting the world go by at a slow pace. You don't have a porch? What a shame! Get yourself a couple of rocking chairs and pretend.

I'm going to find a porch somewhere and sit this weekend with a friend or a neighbor.

Red and yellow, black and white,
they are precious in his sight. Jesus
loves the little children of the world.
—Children's Song

$\mathcal{G}$rowing up in the 1960s, I was very aware of the fact that our country was undergoing a great change. I saw the coverage of the Watts Riots on TV during the long, hot summer of 1965. Images of the civil rights marches in Birmingham and Montgomery and the unforgettable "I Have a Dream" speech by Martin Luther King, Jr. gave my young mind the sense that I was experiencing history in the making.

What did it mean to me in my daily life? I was a white child in a white middle-class neighborhood with virtually no contact with people who weren't like me. Mom and Dad taught me that I was no better than anyone else and that God loved us all the same, no matter what color our skin was. Still, I'll never forget one summer afternoon at the community pool. It was one of those scorching days when it seemed as if every mother within ten miles brought her kids to swim, so the pool was crowded and noisy. That is, until the "Negroes" showed up—a young mother and two boys about my own age. I watched from the side of the pool as the boys slipped out of their T-shirts and into the water.

I shiver when I recall what happened then. Parents motioned to their children to get out of the water, and older kids moved away from the two black boys, leaving them to splash in the water alone. And I recall having this thought: *Will that color come off in the water? I don't want to get any on me.* I'm horrified now to think about it. But I was just a child, and the idea of black skin was strange to me. Three decades later, it makes me wonder, *Do I still harbor any hidden fears and prejudices?* I'm afraid so. Maybe it won't be that way for my kids. At least I hope so.

As I go through my day, I will take notice of my unspoken thoughts and attitude toward those who are different from me, and I will purpose to change the things that are unjust.

> *Then God saw everything that He
> had made, and indeed it was very
> good.*
>
> —*Genesis 1:31*

I've never really thought about what season it was when creation happened. Did the universe begin during the winter, spring, summer, or fall? Or did all the season stuff happen later? Regardless of how you explain the origins of the world, it's kind of fun to hypothesize about what season it was when Adam and Eve were hanging out in the Garden of Eden. I think I can make a pretty good argument for summer, actually. Think about it! It couldn't have been winter because Adam wouldn't have been able to name all the animals. The bears would have been hibernating. And fish are mentioned rather frequently in the story . . . well, you remember that old song, "Summertime, and the livin' is easy, fish are jumpin' and the cotton is high." I rest my case. Not to mention the fact that the first couple were running around buck naked. When is it warm enough to do that, besides summer?

Have I made my point? I realize that there is no mention of watermelon being the forbidden fruit (I don't think God would do that!), and there weren't enough humans around yet to get up a baseball team, but I think Eden sounds like a summer place.

If you're like me, there are probably times during summer when you think you are in paradise, like when the cool breeze comes across the ocean or when the scent of honeysuckle wafts its way onto the front porch on a warm July night.

Ah, creation. Summer showcases it well. And even we can see that it is good.

I will take notice of creation today, and find reasons to agree with God about its goodness.

Familiarity breeds contempt.

Where I grew up, summer meant zucchini. That innocuous little dark-green squash, full of vitamins and minerals, high in fiber, low in fat. Good flavor and good for you. Look for it in the store in January, and you'll pay dearly for all that nutritional value. But come July, if you live in a zucchini-producing area and your neighbors have more than a two-foot square patch of garden, they'll be paying you to take it off their hands.

Forget the fertilizer. Zucchini sprouts forth in great abundance with no help at all. I'm not sure you even have to water it. If you aren't careful, you can grow one as big as a tuba. "Hi, neighbor! How about some fresh zucchini? Just picked it!" Gee, thanks. Mom knew how to cook it, fortunately. Fried zukes, steamed zukes, zucchini bread, zucchini milkshakes . . . you get the picture. By August, if you saw the neighbor coming up the walk with a bulging paper sack, you locked the door and pretended not to be home.

Isn't it funny? In January, we craved fresh zucchini and complained about how expensive it was in the off-season. By the end of the summer, we didn't want to see another green squash as long as we lived.

That's how it is with everything. If we don't have something, we want it. We crave it. Then, when we get it, we lose our desire for it. And if we get too much of it, we soon tire of it and begin to despise it. We've done that with things like a job promotion, recognition, or a relationship. Seems that the rarer something is, the more we value it.

How about some zucchini?

Lord, I will be satisfied with what I have, when I have it.

Sometimes the hardest work to accomplish on a summer's day is the mere act of staying at the task at all, when everything in nature beckons you to come outside and play.

*I*f it weren't for summer rain, I might starve to death. Being self-employed, I'm my own boss, which means that I tend to give myself time off when I need it . . . and sometimes when I don't. When it's clear and warm outside, sometimes it's all I can do to sit down and make myself work. I'd much rather look at the sky and the trees than stare at a computer screen, trying to come up with words. I'd trade my desk for a bike in a heartbeat.

I don't feel that way about winter, unless there's snow falling, in which case I will drop whatever I'm doing. To heck with deadlines! There are snowballs to be thrown! But those days, fortunately for my livelihood, are few. Summer, though, is a different story. I find myself hoping for terrible heat and humidity, so that I won't be tempted to abandon the day's project and head for the park, the pool, or the porch. On fine summer days, when the sky is cobalt blue and there are just a few puffy clouds, every fun thing I've ever done during the months of June, July, and August crowds my mind and screams to be repeated. Let's go to the lake and ski! Get in the car and drive to the beach! Ride bikes in the country! Hike a mountain! Wash the car!

Wash the car? Hey, I'd rather do that than stay inside and work. Wouldn't you?

Can you play hooky from your tasks today, even if for just a few minutes? If not, take five minutes and daydream about something fun you could do if you were outside.

> *Everybody needs his memories, they keep the wolf of insignificance from the door.*
>
> —Saul Bellow

*M*emories are crucial to our existence. Without them, we wouldn't know who we are. Memories give us our own personal history, a history that defines us and gives substance to our being.

But not all memories are good ones. Most of the pain we carry in our daily lives has its roots in memory. For one, it is the memory of sexual abuse by a family member. For another, the memory of a parent who drank too much or was unpredictable in behavior. And for some, the absence of memory is just as significant—the lack of positive interaction with an absent father, perhaps.

Some of us live with the regret of youthful mistakes—having sexual experiences before we were ready, mistreating our bodies with drugs or alcohol, or just wasting time. Even yesterday's mistake is now a memory and part of our history.

As painful as memories can be, they can also be the stepping stones for personal growth. Talking about them with a friend or counselor can help release the grip bad memories often have on our lives. Many times we're not even aware of the hold our memories have on us.

Do unpleasant memories haunt you? Do you find yourself stuffing painful thoughts away that you'd rather not remember? Do yourself a favor and begin to explore that part of your life. It's not easy, but it's worth it in the long run.

Although it is difficult, I will begin the process of opening up with someone about my painful memories.

As Lightning to the Children eased
With explanation kind
The Truth must dazzle gradually
or every man be blind.
—Emily Dickinson

I never really appreciated lightning until I moved to the South. For one thing, it was a rare occurrence in California where I grew up. Once in a while, on a visit to the Midwest, I saw the plains light up with summer storms. And I recall that it was scary, especially because it was always accompanied by loud crashes of thunder. It was the kind of thing that sent kids scurrying for Mom and Dad, usually in tears.

I suppose it helped, hearing that it was "only thunder" or "only lightning" and that it wasn't going to get me. The older I got, I was better able to understand the scientific explanation that lightning had something to do with electricity. There was usually a history lesson with the explanation, something about Benjamin Franklin and a kite with a key attached to the string. You remember that, don't you?

But do you understand it? I don't. Oh sure, I can find out all about the electrical fields and climactic conditions and all that stuff. But there's so much mystery to it. I like the Bible's explana-

. . . .

tion better—about thunder being the voice of God. I don't doubt that for a minute!

What is the truth about lightning and thunder? And how is it that it can be so beautiful, awe-inspiring, and dangerous all at the same time?

Why is there lightning? Why is there love? And pain? I suppose that we won't know the answers to the big questions of life. And that's fine with me.

I can be satisfied with the wonder and mysteries of life, without knowing the answers to all its questions.

. . . .

Do not withhold good from those to
whom it is due,
When it is in the power of your
hand to do so.

—Proverbs 3:27

"I just want you to know that your child was delightful in the nursery this morning." "You have a wonderful way with people, and I admire that." "Your house is so warm and welcoming." "You told that guy the truth on that deal, and I respect you for it."

Wouldn't it be great to hear things like that all the time? How many times do you think about saying something encouraging or uplifting to someone else, but you just don't feel comfortable? It's a risk; what if they think you're just trying to butter them up? You could come off sounding insincere. So you keep it to yourself, instead, and the encouraging word never gets said. Oh, maybe you think about it later and have every good intention of writing a note, but you never get it written. Time goes by and you've lost that moment forever.

It's not just words, of course. There are times when you might see a situation that could use something—time, money, skills—that you possess and could share. It might be as simple as offering to drive an elderly neighbor to the store or washing a friend's car when they're too busy to take care of it. Or it might be a case where you have extra money and know of someone who's struggling financially. What a joy to send an anonymous gift!

Think of the times that someone has given you something right when you needed it—an encouraging note or phone call, a helping hand with a project, or a few bucks when you were strapped for cash. It meant a lot to you, didn't it? Don't miss the opportunity to give to someone else.

Show me, Lord, how I can give of myself to someone else today.

Listen to this, O Job;
Stand still and consider the
wondrous works of God.
—*Job 37:14*

I'll tell you where I'd like to be right now . . . either standing on a peak in the Rocky Mountains or at the shoreline of the Pacific Ocean. Doesn't that sound wonderful? Getting away to a place where nature is right out in front of us can really help to clear our minds of all the stuff that clutters and keeps us from being focused. And it seems to be so much easier to focus on God when we are someplace like the mountains or the beach. The Rockies and the Pacific Ocean would sure qualify as "wondrous works of God," don't you think?

No matter what our religious background, built into each of us is an inward sense that there is Something or Someone bigger than us. In Twelve Step groups, members call on their Higher Power. In the book of Job, God's characteristics are renumerated as Job's friends attempt to counsel him through his trials. Notice that the friend in the story tells Job to "stand still and consider the wondrous works of God."

It's easy to stand still when you're gazing at the Pacific Ocean or breathing mountain air. It's tough to do it when you're in the middle of a crazy work day or surrounded by the demands of a family. But aren't those things also the wondrous works of God? The innocent face of a child, the familiar voice of a spouse, the steadiness and reliability of a co-worker—all these things remind us that we are not alone, that Someone greater is at work in the midst of us. That's a good thing to hold on to when the going gets rough.

Today I will "stand still," if only in my mind, to consider the wondrous things around me.

*When life gives you rain, make
doughnuts.*

I know, it's kind of a goofy twist on "When life gives you lemons, make lemonade," but I like this one better. That's because it really happened, more than once, and it taught me a lesson about adjusting to adverse circumstances. When I was little, we spent quite a few summers at a delightfully ramshackle beach cottage, delightful especially because it was named after me! Our time in that cottage was limited, mostly because my brother and I would get very antsy if we weren't taken down to the water every day. So from morning until sundown, with maybe a break for lunch, those summer days were spent playing in the waves, collecting shells, and building sand castles.

Unless, of course, it rained. Then what? We didn't have a television (for which I am now thankful). I have a hunch Grandma prayed that it would rain so we would stay indoors. "Kids, would you like Grandma to make some doughnuts?" Would we! She'd let us help roll out the dough with her big, wooden rolling pin, and then we'd cut the doughnuts out with the tin mold and drop them carefully into the hot oil. When they cooled, Grandma put them into a paper bag with some sugar and we would shake them until they were covered. Funny how eating a half dozen of Grandma's doughnuts could make an eight-year-old forget about the beach.

Grandma's been gone for years now, but I'll never forget how she could transform a rainy day into something wonderful. And I think I need to get that recipe from Mom.

If I am caught in unpleasant circumstances, I can come up with creative ways to turn them around.

*It hain't no use to grumble and
    complain,
It's jest as easy to rejoice;
When God sorts out the weather
    and sends rain.
Why rain's my choice.*

—J. W. Riley

*T*he morning is rainy where I live, and
though I prefer sunshine to rain most days, I'm
aware of rain's purpose in creation. Where I live,
spring and summer rains are frequent, and the
landscape shows its lovely greening effects in the
light hues of spring to the darker shades of August. Trees are leafy, good for providing shade on
a hot, bright day. If you've seen pictures of Ireland, you know how green it is over there. I
found out why when I visited a few years back. It
rains almost every day, even in the summer. But
it's rarely torrential or violent. Often the rain
comes down in gentle showers or mist, what the
Irish call "soft" days.

Rain does soften the day and quiet the world.
Sun is loud—it just calls for shouting. Notice the
birds; even they are quiet when the rain falls.

Now, I'm one who enjoys a boisterous summer
day, with children laughing and birds chirping
and even cars honking. But it's nice to have a

rainy day every once in a while. It's a good time to get quiet, to be reflective, and to slow down just a bit.

What happens to you on a rainy day? Do you see it as an intrusion, as a foiler of plans or an inconvenience? Or do you accept a rainy day as God's way of getting you to slow down? Rain waters the grass and makes the flowers grow. Can it give some refreshment to your spirit?

Instead of complaining about the rain, I will be thankful and appreciate the way it quiets my world.

Begin to weave, and God will give you the thread.

—German proverb

Some people take great joy in beginning a project. They lay out their tools, line them up neatly, outline the tasks, and set a precise schedule for the work to be done. Then they begin and methodically work through each stage until they finish.

Maybe you're like that, but I'm not. Beginning anything is the worst part because when it comes right down to it, the hardest thing for me is to jump in there and do the first thing on the list.

It just looks so big! And that's any project, whether it's an article to write, a kitchen to clean, or a list of people to call. The task looks enormous, and it threatens to overwhelm me. I'll never get the whole thing done, will I? I'm so thankful that I came upon this little saying: "How do you eat an elephant? One bite at a time." And why? Because there have been too many times in my life when the elephant has eaten *me*. When a task or project is too daunting, I can easily curl up in a little peanut shape and be chomped under the tusks, if you get the picture.

What about you? Is the elephant eating you or are you eating the elephant? It doesn't take much to become a meal for a mammoth. Fear and anxiety rob you of the strength you need to get under way with any task. Mind you, I don't have a handle on it yet, but it's getting better as long as I remember to take it one bite at a time. Besides, trying to eat an elephant at one sitting can make you really sick.

When faced with a project that is overwhelming, I will not be defeated. Instead, I will find satisfaction in completing each small step, until the job is done.

Don't worry about what you missed. You can go back and get it next time around.

—*Charles Wells*

*H*ave you ever seen a combine? It's a piece of farm equipment that combines several functions necessary to the harvesting of grain—reaping, threshing, and winnowing. As the machine drives over an area of wheat, for example, sharp blades cut the heads off the stalks, and the heads are transported to the rear of the machine, where the chaff is winnowed away and the remaining kernels of wheat are conveyed into a holding bin in back.

I sound like a farm girl, don't I? I'm not, but my dad was raised on a farm, as was his dad before him, and on and on back through the generations on that side of my family. So I guess you could say farming is in my blood, which is why I wanted to learn to drive a combine. Fortunately, my farmer uncles were kind enough to oblige me.

It's not easy; a combine doesn't exactly steer like a car, and it's about five times as bulky. And what looks like a flat wheat field often has little bumps and rises in it, which makes the combine weave and shake. Trying to catch all the wheat while cornering is tough for a rookie farmer like me, which meant leaving wide swaths uncut—not a good thing when every kernel means cash.

But my uncles didn't worry about my crooked paths and the precious wheat I left behind. "You'll get it next time," they said. "Just adjust your steering and you'll pick it up."

Sounds like a healthy way to look at life. We can be pretty hard on ourselves if we make a mistake. Wouldn't it be great if we could encourage ourselves and each other that way?

Today, I'll give myself the freedom to make mistakes, knowing that I can go back and do it right the next time around.

He deserves paradise who makes his companions laugh.

There's nothing better than a good laugh. Don't you love being around people who see humor in everyday life? We need to laugh. Even medical science tells us now that laughing is good for us; it releases endorphines, chemicals that get the blood flowing and increase our general sense of well-being. In totally unscientific terms, it feels darn good! Author Norman Cousins wrote about the healing power of laughter in his book *Anatomy of an Illness,* in which he related his battle with disease and his self-administered treatments of Marx Brothers movies and "I Love Lucy" reruns.

You and I may not need a cure for a physical illness, but what about a cure for the summer blahs? Stuck in an office or at home with the kids, sometimes it's hard to see the humor in daily life. Children, of course, can be a great source of laughter. When your kids say something funny, do you let go with a belly laugh or do you hold back? In your work, are you around people who automatically see the funny side of a situation? What about you? Would you be described as someone who has a good sense of humor?

I love what Reinhold Niehbuhr said about laughter. He was an acclaimed theologian, one of the twentieth century's greatest thinkers and the originator of what has become known as the "Serenity Prayer." His advice to those who sat under him? "All you earnest young men out to save the world . . . please, have a laugh."

Isn't that great? We can get so serious about life sometimes that we can wear ourselves—and each other—out. What's your H.Q. (Humor Quotient)? If you're reading this, chances are you're taking a serious look at your own life. That's great. Just let yourself laugh your head off from time to time. Nobody has ever died from an endorphin overdose.

Today, I'll laugh if I feel like it and I won't hold back. I will look for and appreciate the people who make me laugh.

> *"On with the dance, let joy be unconfined"* is my motto, whether there's any dance to dance or any joy to unconfine.
>
> —Mark Twain

I go absolutely nuts when I feel summer coming on. I can't wait until it gets warm enough to wear shorts, and the ice has barely melted off the driveway before I kick off my shoes and go barefoot. I play my stereo several decibels louder between May and October. I drive with the windows down (even if I have to turn the heater on at night) and sing at the top of my lungs. I'm inclined to go a few miles out of my way to "be in the neighborhood" of the local Dairy Dip, just to get a chocolate cone.

What is it about summer? Is it just the weather? That's a lot of it for me. I struggle through the bone-chilling grayness of our long winters. But there's a freedom about summer that just doesn't exist at other times of the year, even during the soft, cheerful spring or the clear crispness of autumn.

Could it be that we can interact with nature in ways that weather prohibits (or at least discourages) at other times? We can run headlong for the surf and dive through a wave, and the cool that greets us is refreshing to body and soul. Flopping down on the sand after a good swim, we feel the tingle of the warm sun against chill-bumped wet skin. Hiking a mountain trail in summer, we work up a healthy sweat and splash ice-cold water on our faces.

Is this making you want to jump up and do something fun? I hope so! There's a lot of joy to be found in summer's pleasures. Let it be unconfined!

Finding joy in small things is a happy, healthy way to live. I'll try it today.

I grow old . . . I grow old . . .
I shall wear the bottoms of my
    trousers rolled.
Shall I part my hair behind? Do I
    dare to eat a peach?
I shall wear white flannel trousers,
    and walk upon the beach.
I have heard the mermaids singing,
    each to each.

—T. S. Eliot,
"The Love Song of
J. Alfred Prufrock"

Growing old is something we all think about. For some of us, those thoughts come more frequently. It's easy to think you're eternally young if you're slim and trim, with a head full of hair. But when those laugh lines around your eyes turn into crevasses and the hair on your head turns silver (some of us wish we had hair at all!), then we're forced to face the reality that we're not teenagers anymore.

Maybe we're seeing the aging process take its toll on our own parents. In our minds, Mom and Dad might be thirty-five, but when we see them now we recognize our grandparents in their maturing faces. Acknowledging that makes us mindful of the fact that we, too, will one day be eligible for senior citizen discounts.

Think about the kind of person you'd like to be twenty, thirty, or forty years from now. Cultivate those life habits and character qualities now. As for me, I hope I'm like J. Alfred Prufrock, walking down the beach wearing rolled-up trousers. I'll dare to eat a peach, and I hope I can hear the mermaids singing, each to each.

Life is a great adventure, from first to last. Help me now, Lord, to become who I'd like to be when I am old.

Think enthusiastically about everything, but especially about your job. If you do, you'll put a touch of glory in your life. If you love your job with enthusiasm, you'll shake it to pieces. You'll love it into greatness, you'll upgrade it, you'll fill it with prestige and power.

—Norman Vincent Peale

*D*o you remember your first job? It was your first taste of real responsibility, of having to be at a certain place at a certain time, of working hard to please a boss who wasn't a parent or teacher. And at the end of the week, there was a real reward—a paycheck with your name on it!

My introduction to the working world was a summer job. It was 1973, and the minimum wage was $1.35 an hour. For that princely sum, I stood behind the counter of Mike's Hero Sandwiches and churned out salami masterpieces all summer, wearing a red, white, and blue outfit to boot. And I learned things that have served me well over the years, things like pride in workmanship (I made the *best* salami sandwiches in town), getting along with co-workers, making the customer happy, and putting a little extra effort into each task—even the boring ones.

Got the summer sluggishness at work? Maybe it's time to remember what that first summer job was like. No doubt you've changed professions since then, but aren't you still the same person, eager to please and anxious to do well? Remember that whatever you do, no one can do it with your unique style and panache. I'll try to remember that myself. One thing for sure . . . it beats slinging salami!

As I go through the day, I will think of which unique strengths I contribute to my job. I will be enthusiastic about my work and bring a "touch of glory" to all I do.

*It goes without saying that you
should never have more children
than you have car windows.*
—Erma Bombeck

$\mathcal{A}$re we almost there? When are we gonna get there? How much longer is it? I have to go to the bathroom." It's the universal language of children on a long car trip. Kids have it a lot easier now, of course. They can put on headphones and listen to music, play a hand-held electronic game—some families even have televisions in their vans.

Maybe it's just the mellowing of years, but I'm glad we didn't have headphones and GameBoys when I was a kid. We didn't have much in the way of entertainment; I'd get carsick, so I couldn't read. Instead we would play word games and listen to Dad point out rock formations and explain the geology of the land as we drove by.

We had a 1963 Ford Fairlane station wagon, white with bright red interior. "White car outside, fire car inside," my little brother called it. We took trips to Wyoming to visit cousins and see Yellowstone; to Disneyland, back when it was surrounded by orange groves; and across the deserts of Utah to Kansas and Grandma's house.

There was no air conditioning, of course. Mom wet towels and stuck them in the windows, and Dad kept a 50-pound block of ice in a Styrofoam cooler so we could suck on ice chips across the desert.

Aren't those wonderful memories? They are now, but I recall I was kind of miserable at the time. I really wish we'd had air conditioning. And, hey, maybe it would have been nice to listen to tapes on my own little Walkman.

But I wouldn't have known about those rock formations and the geology of the western states, or just how good an ice chip can taste when you're in a hot car.

I'll keep the memories I have, thanks.

My memories are precious because they belong to me. Today, I'll take a minute to reflect on something pleasant from my childhood.

> *We must face what we fear; that is
> the case of the core of the restoration
> of health.*
>
> —*Max Lerner*

I remember when I got my first real baseball glove on my ninth birthday in 1966. I had dropped numerous hints about what I wanted— a glove, a softball, and a bat. And on that glorious early summer morning, I flipped on the TV before I went to school. Captain Delta, the local cartoon host, always announced birthdays. Would he say happy birthday to me? Lo and behold, he did! And he told me to look under my bed, where there was a surprise from my mom and dad. I raced there immediately and found a real Spalding glove. It smelled wonderfully of fresh leather, and although it was a little big for my hand, I couldn't wait to play catch with Dad. My goal, you see, was to play in the Bobby Sox girls softball league.

There was only one problem: I was afraid of the ball. Dad would toss one easy, and I would turn away before I could see to catch it. "Just keep your eye on the ball," Dad said. "Put your glove up there—it won't hurt you if you catch it in your glove." I just couldn't shake the fear of getting smashed in the nose. I practiced and practiced, but I always flinched when it came at me.

That's also how I learned to handle conflict. For years, I would look away from a problem, rather than "follow it into the glove." Conflict threatened to smash me, and it was easier to flinch than face it.

I'm better at it now. Not perfect, but better. But it's taken a lot of practice to overcome my fear. I'm playing grown-up softball now, too. And I've made some pretty mean catches at first base.

Fear of being hurt can keep me from addressing conflict. I will look a problem straight on without flinching.

She was a woman of peace, of prayer, and of playfulness.

I got the call when I was in the middle of exams my junior year in college. "Grandma died yesterday." Dad's voice was shaky on the phone. This was the woman who raised him and his eight brothers and sisters on a Kansas farm, and a grandmother of forty.

I hadn't seen Grandma for several years—college and summer jobs had kept me away from the farm. Her funeral was an occasion for this large extended family to gather together, to tell stories and sing songs, to cry some, and to laugh a lot.

Laughing was something Grandma did often. At the funeral service, the priest who attended her in her last days talked about her ability to see the funny side of anything, and he told us a wonderful story that illustrated her character. Having fallen off the bed, Grandma lay there until the nurse happened to come in and notice her. Grandma's only question was "How did the floor get so close to my face?"

That was Grandma. The priest called her "a woman of prayer, of peace, and of playfulness." He'd known her only a short time, but as some-

. . . .

one once said, people tend to die the same way they lived.

Do you ever wonder what people will say about you at your funeral? I would love it if someone said of me what was said of my grandmother. I can't think of a better way to be remembered.

What kinds of things do I want to be remembered for? Starting today, I will nurture the character qualities that I want to develop as I mature.

. . . .

Lives of great men all remind us
We can make our lives sublime,
And, departing, leave behind us
Footsteps on the sands of time.
—*Henry Wadsworth Longfellow*

*A*bout five years ago, I got in line at an automatic cash machine. Taking my place behind the man in line, I caught a whiff of his scent. He smelled just like my grandfather! That scent took me back to the summers when we visited Grandpa and Grandma at the farm, rode the tractors, walked through wheat fields, helped milk cows, and chased prairie dogs in the truck.

But here I was, at a suburban bank, waiting in line for a machine that my grandfather could never have imagined. A machine that gives you money? Grandpa would have clucked his tongue and said, "Wow!"

All those thoughts raced through my mind as I stood behind this man who had the waffled, leathery neck of one who'd spent his life behind the wheel of a tractor. His white hair was cropped short under a feed cap, and he wore his shirt buttoned all the way to the top, just like Grandpa.

And that wonderful smell—it was sweet alfalfa and tractor grease, honest sweat and cow manure, all mixed together in a way that still says "Grandpa" to me.

I stood there at the cash machine, frozen in time. For a moment, I wasn't a grown-up any-more—I was six years old, on Grandpa's knee. I never saw the man's face, but I'm sure it was kind. I wanted to hug him and thank him for bringing back the memory of a man who's been gone for twenty years.

As I remember special people who are no longer with me, I thank you, Lord, for the memories and the positive imprint they left on my life.

He ate and drank the precious
  words,
His spirit grew robust;
He knew no more that he was poor,
Nor that his frame was dust.
He danced along the dingy days,
And this bequest of wings
Was but a book. What liberty
  a loosened spirit brings.
  —Emily Dickinson

*T*ake a walk on the beach on a summer day and what will you find? People stretching out on towels, sitting easy in low chairs, leaning against a cooler. Reading magazines, newspapers, paperback novels, letting the mind take a trip to somewhere else while the sun warms body and soul.

School kids have summer reading lists. While some lose themselves in the pleasure of reading, others are barely able to stay awake, and probably more than half wish they were playing ball instead of reading.

I'm continually torn between the two myself. To celebrate the season, I need to be outside, spending leisure time playing in water somewhere, hiking through the hills, or throwing a ball. But I also love the places that a good book can take me, and I can easily spend an entire summer afternoon in a rocking chair, feet propped up on the porch railing, lost in Faulkner's Mississippi or Conroy's South Carolina coast, Frederick Buechner's Bermuda or Flannery O'Connor's Georgia.

Those who are the least bit introspective or concerned about personal growth are tempted to confine their reading to practical, "self-help" books. But if you're willing to stretch your mind and use that imagination, you can learn a great deal about human nature—especially your own—from a well-written novel or short story. A good book can help you "dance along the dingy days," as Emily Dickinson would say.

I want to stretch my mind and use my imagination. This week, I'll find a good novel and take some time to read.

As a white candle in a holy place,
So is the beauty of an aged face.
—*Joseph Campbell*

We live in a culture that reveres its youth and ignores its elders. Nearly every other culture does the opposite and is the richer for it. We are the poorer for having put our grandparents in retirement villages, far away from grandchildren who don't know the wisdom they are missing by not having Grandpa and Grandma around.

The things we can learn from our elders are limitless. They were born in a time that was very different from our own, and their perspective on life can be of great value as we struggle with our daily lives in this fast-paced, unsettling era. Imagine for a moment: A person born at the end of the last century would have lived through the First World War, the Great Depression, yet another World War, and the suburbanization of America. A telephone would have been a rare thing in the home of their childhood; now their grandchildren can have phones in their cars, their purses, and their pockets.

Life has changed at a speed never seen before in human history. More than ever, we need the sagacity of those who lived in a slower time.

Are the elders all gone from your life? Look

around—people who have lived rich, full lives are sitting near you in a pew, at the train station, and in a nursing home. Ask them questions. Listen, really listen, to their answers. Let them teach you with their stories.

I will listen to the wisdom of the elders around me, and remember the ones who have gone.

*The heavens declare the glory of
  God;
And the firmament shows His
  handiwork.*

—Psalm 19:1

*I*s there any better time of year than summer to go stargazing? Warm nights, crickets chirping, honeysuckle in the breeze, and a big black sky full of stars. You can lie on a blanket on the lawn or in the sand at the ocean or under your sleeping bag on a backpacking trip in the mountains. And to think that on any given night you and I are seeing the same stars—the Big Dipper, Orion, the Pleiades. I can't imagine that anyone could spend a night under the stars and not consider that there might be someone bigger than us, who somehow tossed these diamonds about the heavens. I like what the philosopher Immanuel Kant had to say. "Two things fill the mind with ever new and increasing wonder and awe—the starry heavens above me and the moral law within me."

The stars have inspired Kant, Shakespeare, Van Gogh—what great artist, writer, or poet hasn't used the stars as a subject? Children, lovers, astronomers, and singers find delight in the stars. What about you?

. . . .

When was the last time you gazed into the night sky? The psalmist states that the heavens declare God's glory. Want a wonderful way to contemplate the infinite? Brush up on constellations, take a child outside one night, and show him or her the wonder. "Up above the world so high, like a diamond in the sky . . ." I think you know the rest.

I will look up in the sky tonight and enjoy the wonder of the heavens.

. . . .

The art of leisure lies, to me, in the power of absorbing without effort the spirit of one's surroundings; to look, without speculation, at the sky and sea; to become part of a green plain; to rejoice, with a tranquil mind, in the feast of colour in a bed of flowers.

—Dion Calthrop

*I*f summer is good for anything, it's for developing the art of leisure. These days, leisure is defined as what we do in our spare time, when we're not at work. That can mean anything from mowing the lawn to fixing the car to playing a competitive game of tennis.

All of those things are worthwhile. Mowing the lawn can be relaxing and even fun—so can puttering around under the hood of a car. Working up a good sweat is good for you, whether it's on the tennis court, in the gym, or on the running track.

But what about the fine art of doing nothing? I remember a poster in one of my high school classrooms: "When I work, I work hard; When I sit, I sit loose; When I think, I fall asleep."

I like that philosophy. It implies a healthy approach to life and leisure. Too many of us know good and well how to work hard—we've got the workaholic thing down to a science. Sitting is another thing entirely. Most of us are top-notch pros at "sittin' tight," but "sittin' loose" is not a practiced art.

Maybe it should be. Can you learn to "absorb without effort" the spirit of your surroundings? Can you look at the sky and sea and just enjoy them? Can you let yourself become a part of the scenery without thinking about every little thing that went on at work or at home yesterday? That would be a fine art to learn this summer.

I will develop the art of leisure in a way that frees me from being competitive or task oriented.

I am tired of four walls and a ceiling;
I have need of grass.
—Richard Hovey

One of the finest smells of summer, in my book, is the aroma of new-mown grass. Saturday mornings in June, my windows are open and I hear the familiar drone of a power mower.

Depending on how early it is, and how loud the mower, one of my favorite things is going back to sleep to the hum of that engine. Then, when I finally drag myself out of bed and start the coffee, I walk out on my front porch and catch a whiff of that freshly cut lawn. Ahhh, summer!

Oh, sure. You're thinking that I love the smell of grass because I don't have to mow it! I'd think differently if I had to do it myself every week or so.

Maybe. I guess I missed out on that chore growing up. Not because I was a girl; no, I did mow the grass. It's just that we didn't have very much of it in our California suburb where land was at a premium.

That's why I love mowing my friend's lawn. It's a third of an acre, I guess, and he has a cute little riding mower that goes pretty fast. I pretend

· ·

to be Parnelli Jones on the Indy track, or a wheat farmer on a combine harvesting the grain. I have a great time and it's therapeutic. It amazes me, though, how quickly the grass grows between mowings in the summer. My friend Doug calls more frequently then. "Come on out for some therapy!" I'm glad to do it; it's fun for me, and it frees Doug to spend time with his kids.

Yes, I have need for grass. How about you?

Instead of complaining about a summer chore, I will find a way to enjoy it and have fun.

· ·

I have this big, hungry heart, you see, and nothing here is going to fill it to complete satisfaction. But . . . there are gifts from heaven: dear friends, hot coffee, good books, lightning bugs, watermelon, old houses, and music. And love, always love.

I wrote that in my journal on a day when I was feeling particularly lonely for no one in particular, except for God himself, perhaps. I imagine you have felt those same longings, to know and be known in a way that would touch the deepest places in your soul, those places only you have knowledge of. At times like that, the aching goes so deep that nothing seems to fill it— though we try, don't we? Sometimes the things we use to ease the hunger are destructive, like overindulging in food or alcohol or sex. Other things are more innocuous—spending money or watching TV. Even things that seem to be positive or for the good of someone else can be negative under the surface. We can suck our friends dry or demand more attention from our spouses while it appears that we are doing something for them. It's insidious, really. How can we be sure that our motives are pure?

We can't. But if we are able to recognize the hunger within us for intimacy and love, and realize that it may never be filled completely this side of heaven, then we can be free to enjoy the gifts we do have here—simple things like good books, good friends, and hot coffee.

Father, help me to keep from filling my spiritual emptiness with things that don't satisfy. I will enjoy life's simplest pleasures, knowing that they are gifts from above.

*My advice to you is not to enquire
why or whether, but just to enjoy
your ice cream while it is on your
plate, that's my philosophy.*
—*Thornton Wilder*

*W*arning: this page may cause you to drop
what you're doing, desert your responsibilities,
and head for the nearest soda shop. I am writing
in praise of ice cream, that ambrosia of the gods,
that supreme delight of summer. Dripping from a
cone, served in a paper cup or a crystal goblet,
purchased from a street vendor, or received as a
reward, there is nothing like the feel and taste of
that creamy, cold concoction for bringing a smile
to someone's face.

I was raised to believe that ice cream could
cure anything, and I have no reason to doubt
that. Whether it was a sore finger, an upset stom-
ach, or a broken heart, Dad's remedy was
always a milkshake. Sometimes he'd make it
himself by throwing scoops in a blender, or he'd
just put some in a glass with cold milk and a
spoon and do some vigorous stirring. If the situation was serious, he'd take me down to the
Fosters Freeze, where we'd share a chunky pine-
apple shake in two waxy paper cups.

That might have had something to do with my

crush on a scooper at Baskin-Robbins. The summer of my sixteenth year, I spent fifty-five cents every single day just to get one of his extra-thick jamoca milkshakes. Nothing ever came of the romance, but I've never lost my deep, abiding love for ice cream. Now, if you'll excuse me, I've got to get to the Dairy Queen before it closes.

Today, I'm going to put a smile on somebody's face and buy them an ice cream. Maybe even me.

Each friend represents a world in us, a world possibly not born until they arrive, and it is only by this meeting that a new world is born.

—Anaïs Nin

*W*hat a lovely thought! By the time we're adults, most of us have made so many friends that we have a universe of worlds that enrich our lives, interweaving and creating a prism of relationships that bring lovely colors and patterns to our lives.

It's not often that we take the time to consider the building blocks of relationships, or the things that a particular friend brings to our lives.

And think of all the other people you now care about, because they are important to your friend. Our friendship worlds expand exponentially as we grow in relationships, as their friends become ours.

Wonderful, isn't it?

I will take stock of my closest of friendships, and be thankful for the worlds I have known because of them.

> As imperceptibly as Grief
> The Summer lapsed away . . .
> And thus, without a Wing
> Or service of a Keel
> Our Summer made her light escape
> Into the Beautiful.
>
> —Emily Dickinson

I dread this time of year, as summer draws to a close. It starts with the back-to-school ads in the newspapers, and soon the high school bands are practicing in the afternoon. And though the heat of summer may wear on through October in some parts of the country, Labor Day weekend is the traditional end of the vacation season.

I hate it. School is back in session (a certain relief for many parents!). Although my life doesn't change just because school starts, I feel that familiar sense of summer's end. Playtime is over; time to go back to work.

I don't want to! Don't make me! I want summer to last and last. I want to take another trip to the beach, another spin around the lake, one more dive in the pool. I want to stay in my shorts and T-shirts, and I don't want to get my cool weather clothes out of storage just yet. I haven't finished my summer reading list! I didn't perfect my golf swing or my tennis game. I didn't visit my family enough. I didn't eat enough ice cream or drink enough lemonade or spit as many watermelon seeds as I wanted to.

Summer is always too short for me. But I'll let it go, eventually, and embrace once again the particular pleasures of fall. I'm just glad I had one more summer, aren't you? I'll carry its memories with me into the next season.

Knowing that summer is coming to a close, I will cherish the times I enjoyed with family and friends.